PICTURE FRAMING

A Practical Guide from Basic to Baroque

PICTURE FRAMING

A Practical Guide from Basic to Baroque

Desmond MacNamara

David & Charles
Newton Abbot London North Pomfret (Vt)

©DESMOND MAC NAMARA 1986
BRITISH LIBRARY CATALOGUING IN
PUBLICATION DATA

Mac Namara, Desmond
    Picture Framing: a practical guide from
    basic to Baroque
    1. Picture Frames and Framing   Amateurs
    manuals
    749´7   N8550

    ISBN 0-7153-0205-1 P/B

First published 1986
Reprinted 1992
First published in paperback 1994
Reprinted 1996, 1999

Designed by Laurence Bradbury

Printed in the Netherlands by Royal Smeets
Offset BV, Weert

CONTENTS

INTRODUCTION

THERE HAVE BEEN many books on practical picture framing, published in Britain and America. The best of them emphasize the importance of proportion, choice of mouldings, textures, colour and finishes, and make some effort to point the reader in an imaginative direction. Others, alas, offer little more than advice on chopping up bits of ready-made moulding and assembling them into rectangles, or cutting holes in sheets of board – the least part of the whole business. A well-framed picture on which thought and skill have been lavished should have double the sensual impact of a picture neatly boxed by a competent local framer. The difference is not a matter of cost, as I hope to show. Quite the reverse. The added factor is made up of judgment, knowledge, invention and the few dozen tricks that underlie the practice of any art. I can only point to the former and attempt to explain something of the latter.

When, by chance as much as anything, I first undertook to teach picture framing to adults, I quickly realized that there was little to teach except some specialized carpentry and the rudiments of taste and proportion. When I tried to extend this I came up against the high cost of mouldings, inconvenient expeditions to specialized shops and difficult choices. Many of the mouldings that satisfied my criterion were beyond the pockets of my students and were in any case pitifully few in number. When someone brought a tolerable copy of a Goya pastoral, no one could supply the elements of a Spanish baroque frame which would have made the picture a striking mural event.

I began to break this tyranny of supply by guiding some students to frame a few National Gallery Italian renaissance prints in an appropriate manner, using simple pieces of timber from a DIY shop and some gesso, colour and so forth. The main tool, apart from saw, hammer etc., was a sharp stylus made from a 2-inch (50-mm) nail for engraving the chaste design in gesso on the centre flat area (a piece of two-by-one/50 × 25-mm timber) with the help of a stencil cut in a strip of copper. When it worked, the excitement it engendered in the class drove me to exploring available public collections of paintings to see if I could extend my capacities.

I cannot pretend that I enjoy all the framing in the great national collections, but I saw many mouldings which could not be bought but which my students would be eager to use if this were remotely possible. I also realized that some speeding up of traditional methods was needed for students who only spent a few hours a week in my company. Many traditional materials and methods could not be bettered and had to be used, but some could be advantageously adapted, although not improved, by using modern sculptural techniques. This principle came to me one day when I began to think of a frame moulding as a narrow sculptural or architectural frieze.

From the 15th century to the third quarter of the 18th century nearly all frames were carved in wood, but there were exceptions. Added ornament in a sort of stucco composition was described in detail by Cellino Cellini in the 15th century, cast from terra cotta reverse moulds. In the 16th century in Italy, and probably in France, reproduced designs of this kind were used in small framing and in the elaborate theatrical occasions, masques and the like, which were part of royal or ducal weddings – acres of painted backdrops, triumphal arches, temples, statues, gods, chariots and costumes, enlivened by ballets of naked nymphs and tritons.

In the second half of the 18th century in France, carved wooden frames were chiselled very roughly in soft wood and coated heavily with gesso which was itself carved and sharpened by specialists. At about the same time the practice of adding ornament in *papier maché* and gesso composition began to spread, with the effulgence of rococo ornament. This produced an anti-French backlash in England on the part of English designers like Johnson and Chippendale, both of whom were notable frame designers as well as furniture makers. But the process of adding ornament was too economic to be a passing fashion, and the increasing demand for framing on the part of the middle class in Europe throughout the 19th century meant that the practice had come to stay.

When seeking to enlarge the repertoire of moulding designs for my students, I was downcast at the number of elegant and useful patterns made by good craftsmen long since dead, and sought to find some way of revitalizing their ghosts. This had to be done in such a way that it could be carried out within the confines of a class, without subdivisions of labour or inordinately lengthy apprenticeships. In the pursuit of this aim, I discovered that some repeating patterns on mouldings could be copied, in clay or wax, given some modelling skill. One unit of design might be no more than a few inches long, and several casts of this, joined length to length and patched at the joints, produced a length of moulding about 3 feet (1 m) long, a convenient length for storing. By the same token an agreeable and suitable design could be abstracted from a Chinese urn, a Persian tile or a New Guinea bark cloth and reassembled as a running pattern for a picture frame moulding that a Sung Chinese or a Persian miniaturist would not have envizaged, but would instantly recognize.

In the pages that follow I attempt to describe the result of these endeavours, starting from four pieces of timber and utilizing some extremely decorative period mouldings with a variety of finishes, largely of my own devising. The repair or reconstruction of damaged frames is also described, using a combination of new materials with those that have proved their superiority for more than five hundred years.

I make no bones about the fact that I am describing a hundred or so conjuring tricks, mostly but not all of my own devising, and can only point the way towards experience and aesthetic judgment. For a beginning I can only recommend visits to national collections. Some knowledge of the history of Western art is invaluable, indeed essential, but this is acquired gradually. Hopefully the quest will prove exciting. Everything described has been fully tested with adult students of very mixed ability, and they all work, sometimes spectacularly well. This book has to confine itself to the subject, perforce

Leonardo Da Vinci (1452–1519). La Gioconda. This is the last of several frames lost during thefts, but it is correct for the turn of the 16th century: the later Renaissance

narrowly, so I cannot include a chapter on devising a new moulding design. I know, however, that some readers will have some skill in this direction and I have attempted to show them how to use and adapt it. A picture frame or a mirror glass frame is really linear sculpture, deriving from architectural design and echoing the furniture of a given period.

Sadly, too many people, including some who should know better, have a very sketchy understanding of the development of framing down the centuries. Some knowledge of its historical development needs to be balanced against other criteria, such as aesthetic judgment, ambience and mother wit, in deciding how to frame a painting, a drawing or any flat image. Fashion, like the law, is 'an ass', as Charles Dickens described it; nonetheless it merits considerable respect. Simplicity in itself is not a merit, as a generation of architects has discovered, nor is overloaded design. Prejudice in both of these directions is common and obscures good judgment.

The practice of picture framing is now world-wide but this is a fairly recent development. It developed in Europe over the last five hundred years from architectural design, of which it is a part. Elsewhere in the world, sophisticated schools of painting developed which did not involve framing or hanging pictures on walls. Apart from fresco painting on lime plaster walls, Persian, Chinese, Japanese, Indian or Mogul paintings were not hung. Some were kept in folios, some stored in chests, to be taken out and enjoyed on suitable occasions. Nowadays, social habits having changed, all such precious objects would be safely framed and displayed or, I fear, locked away in a bank vault.

Early examples of framing

Since no classical panel painting remains, apart from the encaustic Roman mummy portraits found at Fayum, Egypt, there is no evidence of framing. However, many of the fresco panels painted on the walls of Pompeii and nearby cities are surrounded by light and dark lines resembling some 17th-century gallery frames. There are examples of small fresco panels framed in stucco cornices remarkably resembling frames carved in wood.

Examples of these are numerous. There is a wall panel of Orpheus charming the beasts in mosaic in the Palermo Museum. It is surrounded by a mosaic 'frame' of a twisted rope pattern set on a flat between an inner and outer ridge. Executed in wood, such a frame was common from the 17th century onwards. In the Naples Museum there is a landscape panel from Herculaneum 'framed' in a painted red border of three red lines, like many 17th-century gallery frames. A small relief of the building of the ship Argo from the Villa Albani is framed in an oval beading in stucco that would not have seemed out of place in the court of Louis XVI.

But there are endless such examples. When we consider that many architectural features in classical times were stone developments from wooden originals, and that painting was a cheap form of sculpture, it seems reasonable to assume that when we look at these 'frames' in mosaic, stucco or fresco, we are looking at representations of wooden frames.

The panel painting did not play a large part in classical art, nor did it in the centuries that followed the fragmentation and collapse of the Roman Empire, but the idea of a decorative border around a manuscript painting was common.

The Irish monks of Iona adapted Christian symbols to the whorls and convolutions that their ancestors had used for centuries, and the decorative border was a common feature of their extraordinary art. The St. John page of the 9th-century Book of Kells shows the saint, highly conventionalized, but surrounded by a border which, remarkably, resembles the rhythms and proportions of a 17th-century baroque frame; a Louis XIV corner and centre ornaments are identical. This is coincidence, but whether on vellum or on plastered walls, the idea that a painted image of a scene that emanates from an artist's mind needs a boundary line or border to enclose it seems deeply ingrained in European culture. The world of the painter's imagination cannot be allowed to sprawl onto the hewn stone blocks of reality and must be contained within a border.

A SHORT HISTORY OF PICTURE FRAMING

THIS BRIEF SUMMARY of the history of European framing is intended as a guide, a synopsis of the subject, useful to students visiting national collections in any country, from Edinburgh to Rome. Its purpose is to suggest the evolution in painting and taste and to draw attention to the fact that there is a vast reservoir of design to be understood, adapted or taken into account. The more you know the better your judgment.

Early panel paintings in the 13th and 14th centuries were votive and often in triptych form: a painting with a centre panel and two hinged side panels with a major and two subsidiary subjects as in the Duccio Madonna from the National Gallery, London. These were small enough to be portable and often used for portable altars.

In the 15th-century panel painting had become more fashionable and advanced in technique. It is at this time that framing developed in two different directions, and the results of this are still in evidence today. In Flemish merchant towns like Bruges or Ghent a realistic school of painting with a linear style developed, featuring religious subjects for altar use and secular portraits. The secularization of treatment, even for religious purposes, was essential to advance the art of painting past the static imagery of the icon or the mosaic.

Robert Campin (1387–1455). Early Flemish painter. The simple moulded frames matched the panelled houses of the merchant class of that time (National Gallery)

These northern painters set their work in very simple wooden mouldings, ideally suited to the panelled merchants' homes, churches and almshouses in which they hung. The portrait by Robert Campin (1387–1455) and the 'Man in a Turban' by Jan van Eyck (1390–1441) from the National Gallery, London both exemplify this, but the suitability of this light Flemish framing is instantly apparent if one visits the Memling Museum or the Hôpital St. Jean by the intersecting canals of Bruges in Belgium, a city like the coloured toyland of a Gothic illuminated manuscript.

In Italy, the Dominican monk Fra Angelico (1387–1445) was a contemporary of Campin. His style, though tender, was very conservative by Florentine standards. Nevertheless, the difference in mood and scale between Flanders and Tuscany can be seen by anyone immediately. A generation later the whole drift of Renaissance taste is more apparent. Still Gothic in feeling and paid for by trade, the framing of the 'Madonna della Rondine' by Carlo Crivelli, the Venetian painter (c. 1430–95) reflects a different world; not better or worse but imbued with classical pretensions which perhaps never died in Italy. This kind of early Renaissance frame is called an 'aedicula' from the Latin 'aedes', a public building; a Roman dolls' house for a Virgin and a swallow.

Within a few decades the pilasters had shrunk to low relief, the cornice had disappeared and a recognizable modern frame had developed, consisting of an outer and inner narrow moulding and a broader centre flat. The frame on the 'Portrait of a Girl', Studio of Domenico Ghirlandaio (1449–1494) has a broad flat decorated with a remarkably modern running leaf pattern. This useful and handsome class of frames can still be used with a modern or period finish and is very easy and cheap to make. In the 15th century the centre flat area was often painted in classical volutes, rosettes and the like, or had slightly raised ornament of gesso laid on with a brush.

The latter half of the 16th century was an epoch of prodigious invention and discovery of Shakespeare and Michelangelo and the conquest of Mexico and Peru. Painting and architecture, particularly in Italy, had overcome many obstacles. In Rome and Florence painting and related design became less enterpreneurial and more governed by aesthetic and philosophical theory. Painters were given to elongation of figures and small heads. It became much more secular in subject matter and quite frequently was sexual in subject matter, in an astringent sort of way. 'Leda and the Swan', for instance, was a typical subject.

Colours became more strident with sharp yellows, pinks and

Duccio di Buoninsegna (1260–1319). Madonna triptych. Duccio was the founder of the Sienese school which was partly responsible for the initiation of picture framing (National Gallery)

greens. El Greco, trained in Venice under Titian, was typical, although his favourite framing derived from the late 15th-century style, with a broad centre flat, but unadorned and painted a dark colour, commonly green. Yellow ochre was used to replace gold, possibly to avoid a colour clash. This period is known in English as 'Mannerist' from the Italian 'Gran Maniera'. Tintoretto, the later Michelangelo and above all Parmigianino were exponents of this search for novelty and the extreme gesture of nude figures (*contraposto*). By the end of the 16th century the intimations of baroque rhythms are evident in painting, the ornamental use of the scallop shell, the nautilus (or snail) shell and the half figure, ending up in a foliage pilaster from the groin downwards, became fashionable. In framing, the designs were very varied, heavy architectural invention, forcefully applied predominated, but it could be more restrained.

In the north a generation later, in Protestant Holland and Catholic Antwerp, the two greatest painters, Rembrandt van Rijn (1606–69) and Peter Paul Rubens (1577–1640) still derived, if that is a fair word, from the Mannerist tradition, and their framing was rich and heavy. Shown below is a sketch by Rembrandt for the framing of his 'Anatomy Lesson of Dr. Deyman' (Ryksmuseum) in 1656. This was intended for the Amsterdam Anatomical Theatre, not a private house. Domestic framing or 'gallery framing' in private or even ducal collections was much simpler. The painting of the 'Cognoscenti' (Nat. Gall. London), shows the duality in taste between northern and Italianate fashions in the 1620s.

The painting 'The Guitar Player' (Iveagh Bequest, Kenwood House, London, on page 13) by Vermeer of Delft (1632–75) shows externally and internally two very typically 17th-century frames, one peculiarly Dutch and one more generally used. The real frame is cut in walnut with a variety of wave patterns and highly polished. Ebonizing was also popular. Such severely rectangular frames in decorative woods with subtle textural carving continued in popularity until the 1930s, but they were originally a valiant attempt at native Protestant sensuality, deeply suspicious of Italian Papist exuberance and the 'Jesuit inspired' flamboyance of the Counter Reformation. The frame on the landscape in the painting is ornamented and gilded and has hints of the baroque style to the extent that there is an emphasis on a heavier corner ornament, a device that developed towards the end of the century and became in a looser, more organic way one of the most characteristic features of the more curvacious, more feminine Rococo style by the 1720s. The painter Watteau bridges both styles in frames, but belonged heart and soul to the latter.

First used derogatively, the word 'baroque' is said to derive from the Portuguese for a misshapen pearl, such as were fashionable for miniature sculptures in the guise of jewellery, earrings and the like.

As a style in any of the arts, baroque had a serene certainty, but it had equally a restless waywardness which encouraged a tendency towards surprises, particularly in architecture. It was extremely abstract, although the elements that were distorted were all of classical origin. The extent to which it was the particular expression of the Roman reaction to Protestant Europe is less important than its capacity to adapt to different societies. St. Paul's in London, designed by Sir Christopher Wren (1632–1723) is certainly baroque, but in an austere northern way which seems far removed from the

Rembrandt Van Rijn (1606–69). Rembrandt had two 'Anatomy Lesson' commissions. This is his draft sketch of the frame for 'The Anatomy Lesson of Dr Deyman'; a heavily enshrined painting for the Amsterdam Anatomical Theatre (Ryksmuseum)

'The Guitar Player' by Jan Vermeer (1632–75) in Kenwood House, showing two 17th-century frames. One, outside the painting is characteristically Dutch, while the frame within the painting is more in the French style (Victoria and Albert Museum)

theatrical effulgence of the Piazza Navona in Rome by Bernini (1598–1690), the great master of the style.

In framing, baroque was able to contain many degrees of opulence or simplicity. The pictures on pages 14–17 show an anglo-Dutch frame from Ham House by the Thames, a Spanish baroque frame, and a Grinling Gibbons (1648–1721) from the Victoria & Albert Museum.

The Spanish baroque frame shares with French frames the claim to be the most perfect product of the craft of framing. Its dark background colour and its muted ornament make it one of the great pleasures of the Prado Museum in Madrid. The Velasquez 'Lady with a Fan' (Wallace Collection, London, see page 15) gives a good idea of its sombre sensuality. Ideal for certain portraits, it is a fairly easy frame to build from scratch.

Rococo was a sinuous, curvacious development from baroque, a baroque shorn of its political pretensions and assumption of autocratic power. It was essentially a French style, though of course it spread to many countries, most comfortably in Germany and more superficially (although fashionably) in England. Cabinet-makers like Johnson and Chippendale were responsible for very elaborate rococo picture and glass frames in the 'Chinese' style and the 'Gothic' style, both English.

task to enrich this frame in various textures, tones, colour washes, silver or gold both to transform it and to learn fundamental techniques in the process. These will be described in Chapter 5. The main purpose of making such a basic frame, however, is to combine a number of techniques without much expense or frustration. I have used it in teaching for many years and found it very effective.

All made-up mouldings are cut and joined in the manner described above, though narrower mouldings are always more difficult to handle. A common mistake is to use too narrow a moulding for a large area of glass. The tiny contact points at the corners are not very strong and disasters happen after a year or two in a dry atmosphere. In general, there seems to be a widespread puritan fear of any generosity in frame dimensions. The frame should be appropriate, neither simple nor elaborate.

Most beginners and many more experienced framers will expect to use factory-made mouldings. Some are well designed, particularly if they are purchased from a good stockist, but many on sale are 'plastic' and meretricious.

Clockwise from top left: A plastic Stanley mitre block, a wooden mitre block, and a Marples mitre guide operated from the side on which the screws are situated

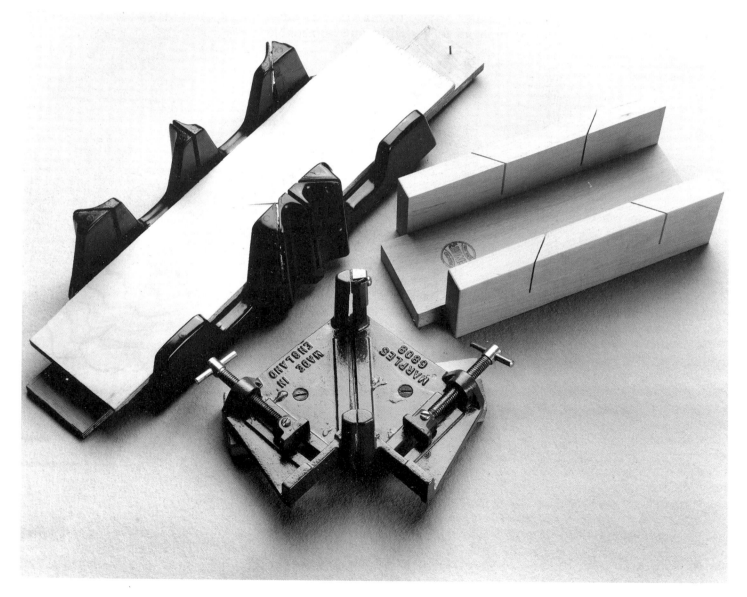

Choice is a matter of judgment, taking account of colour, texture and width. Offensive and garish 'gold' finishes can be stippled with brown gouache in size as described elsewhere and wax polished. Bruised corners can be filled with tinted wax or warmed wax crayons of appropriate colour. Wax gold amalgam can be used as a filler and polished when dried hard.

There are techniques for cutting and joining mouldings other than those just described. A U-shaped wooden mitre-block can be used, holding the moulding against the far wall of the trough. Wooden mitre blocks are the oldest, and have been used for at least five centuries. They are quite satisfactory, provided you keep a strong grip to keep the length of moulding from jumping. The Stanley tool manufacturers make a plastic mitre block based on the wooden one. It needs the addition of a flat piece of wood into which the saw teeth can cut after passing through the moulding, and also a base strip with a piece of two-by-one (50 × 25-mm) to form a T-structure to fit in a vice. The saw slots are rather loose, perhaps due to the plastic casting methods, but it is possible to glue a strip of mounting board inside

A wide variety of commercially made mouldings is available in many different finishes and sizes

you, slowing down as you near the farther pin prick and looking into the chimney where the blade can be seen until it fractionally crosses the pin prick.

18. Turn the board around clockwise and start again with the straight-edge, the tool and the distance gauge and cut the second side, and so on. Always keep a firm pressure on the tool, as with a knife, and hold the free end of the straight-edge firmly with the free hand.

It looks very complicated spelled out in words, but it only takes about fifteen minutes.

A few practice runs on a spare piece of board will quickly put flesh on the bones of theory. If the centre of the mount window does not come away with a sharp tap, the corners may need releasing with a sharp knife, held at the appropriate angle.

It should be noticed that in the entire process of measuring a picture, estimating and cutting a mount, it has not been necessary to use a ruler. The complications that flow from double or treble measurements, adding and subtracting and increasing the field of error, are avoided. It does assume the physical presence of the picture, but this should always be the case. A costume designer must have physical reference to age, sex and occasion, and similar considerations apply to pictures and paintings.

The art of mounting (or matting) a picture involves complex matters of judgment and aesthetic choice. Latent capacities in both of these are best extended by visiting private galleries and the better group exhibitions. National collections sometimes tend to be very conservative.

White board is usually more brilliant than the white paper of a print or drawing, and a light ivory may prove more flattering. While all aesthetic rules need to be broken at times, in general a mount, or a frame for that matter, may well echo a colour in the picture, but not in the same tone. A dominant blue in a watercolour is better matched by a blue-grey board than a blue one. Heavy drawings or woodcuts with large areas of white often look well with a charcoal brown board. All the greys are useful, warm or cold (a touch of yellow or blue). Before deciding on a cream mount, for instance, give a thought to one of the light greys which sometimes look both restful and striking.

Black should be used sparingly, though it can be very enhancing at times. Remember that the colour of a board lies in a thin sheet of paper pasted over it. The darker colours, brown, black, dark green, tend to tear slightly if the cutting blade is not surgically sharp. Occasionally a 'rogue' board occurs in which the colour paper is not fully united to the board. Discard all such.

The preceding instructions were concerned purely with measuring and cutting the card, a difficult enough task for a beginner. But there are at least six sub-species in the mounting category which need some comment.

A *double mount* consists of two window openings, the inner one smaller than the outer one, and usually of a different colour or tone. First the outer limits are defined and cut, and then the precise positioning of the inner mount. Both mounts are then cut with great care for slight variations in parallel will show up badly.

The *lining of mounts* with the addition of bands of colour wash or gold is really a piece of period pastiche and it seems to me that it should be limited to a water-colour style common in the *belle époque* or topographical prints of the same period or whenever it is thought appropriate to suggest the *fin de siècle* or the turn of the century.

The lining is traditionally done with suitable drawing nibs from an art shop and Indian ink, though many will find modern waterproof

A variety of samples of lining and colouring

Far left: Samples of mount lining, seen here with a period wash drawing

Left: An abstract expressionist wash drawing with a canvas covered mount

Below: A topographical engraving showing a lined mount

A flat textured frame and textured mount in different colours, contrasting an Indian enamel picture on copper

Gesso texturing can be used not only on mounts, but just as effectively on wood, plain mouldings or parts of mouldings, and hardly ever fails to make the surface more interesting, without interfering with the painting. With acquired deftness it is possible to simulate, cheaply but durably, the feeling of linen, fossilized stone, bronze, copper in any key, high or low as might be thought supportive and flattering. These latter are the only criteria, in equal measure.

Tools are needed, but they need to be acquired or made as often as not, rather than bought. Plastic nail brushes, plastic throwaway toothbrushes or the coarser plastic scrubbing brushes are excellent. They can be sawn or cut into small sections to suit easy handling. One of my best texturing tools is a tiny plastic hairbrush from a doll's toilet set, coaxed by a student from a small girl.

An interesting effect can be obtained by painting on a second coat of gesso on the mount board, having previously sized it and given it one coat of gesso. Paint a rich coat of gesso on one side of the mount, overlapping two corners (see illustration). Wait a few moments for the gesso to gel, and firmly score it with a piece of plastic nail brush or whatever, in any suitable way. Sloping the strokes to the corner is effective, but so is a fish scale pattern of overlapping half-circles. If the gesso dries too much, quickly slap on some more on the half-dried area and proceed right round the margins of the board. The part in the centre which is yet to be cut out can be left bare, but generously overlap its edges. If the lines begin to join up after scratching, the fresh gesso is still too liquid so wait a further thirty seconds.

The scratched (*sgraffito*) lines need not, and indeed should not be exactly uniform. Strive for a general effect as in painting. Leave it to dry for an hour and a colour wash can be applied if needed. Colour washes are in this instance best made from a dab of gouache colour in a small warmed saucer of thin rabbit glue, a transparent tempera. Test out the strength on white paper and thin further or deepen as needed. Spread a generous brushful on some newsprint and dry it, the lettering should be legible. Using a good large hog brush, paint it on quickly, without stopping until the entire surface is covered, and leave to dry. Any lingering will soften the gesso and produce a ghastly mud. Indeed the whole process should be done with speed and

Texturing a mount with a plastic nailbrush in wet gesso

Mount

Textured surface

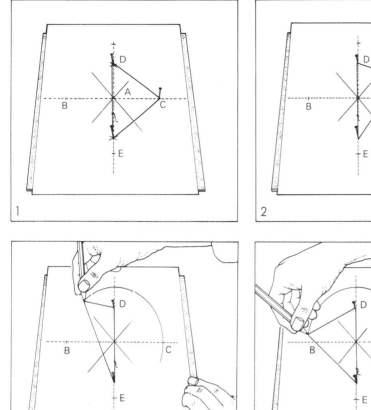

The process of drawing an oval of predetermined size

Top left: Thread the loop around the located pins

Top right: A pencil replaces the pin and the arc then follows the confining thread loop

Bottom left: Continuing the oval contour

Bottom right: The oval half completed.

hopeful certainty, just like a gouache sketch or a wash drawing.

To cut a *circular or oval mount*, a hardboard template is needed, cut with a band-saw and with smooth edges. These can be stored until a 'library' of sizes is acquired for subsequent re-use. Circles are drawn with compasses, but the more commonly used oval is more complex.

The mounting card, cut to size and exactly rectangular, is laid on the cutting board and the centre point established by getting the crossing point of the two diagonals with a ruler. Only pencil the central 'x' of the two crossing lines (see illustration). Using a set-square on one side and a ruler passing through A, tick off half the width of the desired oval with a pair of compasses at points B and C. In a similar way, setting the compasses at half the height of the oval, tick off D and E. With the compasses still set at half the height, set the point at C and describe a short piece of arc above and below A. Set the compasses from B and describe two similar arcs cutting the first two. At the point where these arcs cross, lightly hammer in two 1-inch (25-mm) moulding pins, through the mounting board and securely into the cutting board. Drive a similar moulding pin into point C. Tie a loop of cotton lightly around the base of the three pins, but without any slack. If the knot is fixed with a blob of quick-drying cement it will keep them from slipping. Remove the pin C and substitute a pencil, and allow it to follow its tethered path around the board. The result will be an oval of predetermined size and proportion, wide or narrow, as illustrated.

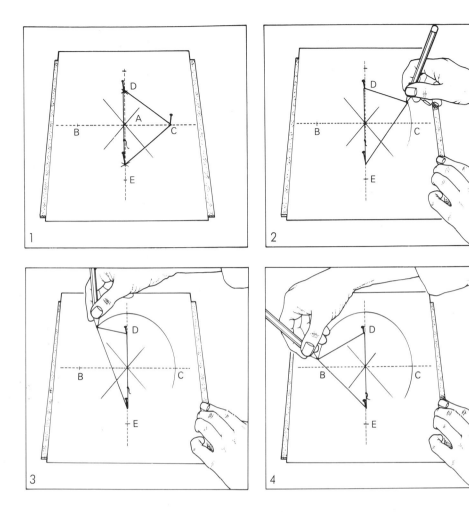

The process of drawing an oval of predetermined size

Top left: Thread the loop around the located pins

Top right: A pencil replaces the pin and the arc then follows the confining thread loop

Bottom left: Continuing the oval contour

Bottom right: The oval half completed.

hopeful certainty, just like a gouache sketch or a wash drawing.

To cut a *circular or oval mount*, a hardboard template is needed, cut with a band-saw and with smooth edges. These can be stored until a 'library' of sizes is acquired for subsequent re-use. Circles are drawn with compasses, but the more commonly used oval is more complex.

The mounting card, cut to size and exactly rectangular, is laid on the cutting board and the centre point established by getting the crossing point of the two diagonals with a ruler. Only pencil the central 'x' of the two crossing lines (see illustration). Using a set-square on one side and a ruler passing through A, tick off half the width of the desired oval with a pair of compasses at points B and C. In a similar way, setting the compasses at half the height of the oval, tick off D and E. With the compasses still set at half the height, set the point at C and describe a short piece of arc above and below A. Set the compasses from B and describe two similar arcs cutting the first two. At the point where these arcs cross, lightly hammer in two 1-inch (25-mm) moulding pins, through the mounting board and securely into the cutting board. Drive a similar moulding pin into point C. Tie a loop of cotton lightly around the base of the three pins, but without any slack. If the knot is fixed with a blob of quick-drying cement it will keep them from slipping. Remove the pin C and substitute a pencil, and allow it to follow its tethered path around the board. The result will be an oval of predetermined size and proportion, wide or narrow, as illustrated.

Right: Two enamel paintings with textured mounts in mid-Victorian and fin de Siècle Japanese styles

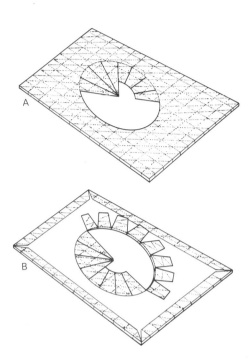

Many oval mounts were covered in silks, velours and linens. The cloth is cut and applied as shown above

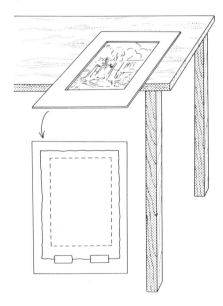

Aligning the print in the mount and, on the back, the initial fixing with gummed tape

It is difficult to cut an oval by hand, but it is possible. A Dexter cutter will do the job, but a template in hardboard must be cut, smaller than the desired oval by the width of the mark on the card gauge. The whole cutting board with the lightly pinned mounting card needs to be revolved during parts of the cutting, particularly at top and bottom and the template, which needs to be pinned down through to the cutting board, rakes the place of a straight-edge. Most frequently an oval mount is needed for a period picture or vignetted photograph, and can be coevered with a fabric, usually an exotic one like velvet. In this case a non-bevelled cut will serve, and a little uncertainty around the edge will not show. The covering of an oval mount is similar to a rectangular one except for the inside lapover of the fabric, which should be as shown.

Papers can be pasted to mounting boards to obtain certain subtle effects of texture or even colour. This can be done as with a fabric. Many papers stretch when wet and subsequently shrink, which bows the mounting board, and a counter paper is needed on the back to even out the stresses. After pasting with a flour or cold water paste, the card should be placed under a board with a weight on top. Good paper shops sell a variety of imitation and real hand-made papers which can be very attractive. Modern spray-on paper adhesives in aerosols can be bought. The particular directions should be followed or adapted. Beginners should not expect instant results. Tricks can be taught but confidence and style come more slowly.

To make an even flour paste, shake a tablespoon of white flour to cover the bottom of a small saucepan and trickle in two tablespoons of cold water, stirring with a hog brush into a smooth cream without lumps. Now add eight tablespoons (120 ml) of cold water, mix, and stir with the brush over a low flame until it has bubbled for about 30 seconds. A few drops of any phenolic antiseptic or half a teaspoon (2·5 ml) of boracic acid crystals added before heating inhibits fungus growth in the event of later humidity.

When taping a paper picture to finished mount, never use a self-sticking tape. These behave disastrously after a few years, and Sellotape is catastrophic. Always use gummed paper tape that needs wetting. This will do no harm to the paper of the painting and is very strong. Even after fifty years it can be removed, by brushing it with water, waiting a few minutes and peeling it off.

Water-colours, usually uneven from the washes, often need a gentle damping on the back with a wrung-out sponge, but never too wet. After fixing the result will sag like a sail in a doldrum, but will tauten and shrink in drying.

To align the picture to the mount window, avoid a ruler whenever possible. Lay the picture over the edge of the table by a few inches and position the mount on top of it. Very fine visual adjustments can be made. Then, holding the picture and mount steady with a spread hand, stick two postage stamp pieces of gummed tape underneath on either side of the base of the back of the picture and onto the back of the card. You have to bend down to see what is happening. Wait ten seconds and turn the board over.

Stick an overlapping strip of gummed paper all round, from one side to its opposite, and attempting to stretch slightly. If it goes wrong, paint the gummed strip with clean water, wait a few moments and it will peel away. Most synthetic tapes or adhesives tear the paper on attempting to remove them.

Competent mounting can be learned in about twelve hours and as many again to gain experience. It is a subtle business in which the cutting and preparation of the mount are the easiest part. Imagination can take over when confidence disolves its constraints.

Aligning the print visually and securing with gummed tabs

Print and mount face down showing the gummed tabs

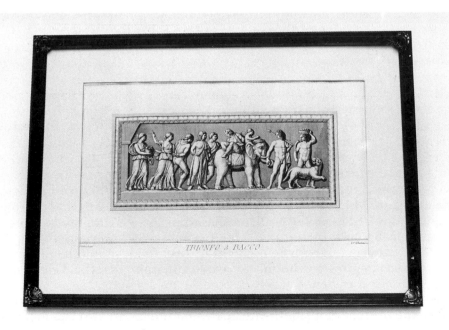

Gummed paper tape securing the print to the mount

Left: A mid-18th-century engraving mounted and framed in a discrete period style for library or study

REPRODUCING FROM ANTIQUE MOULDINGS

I HAVE ALREADY mentioned how cast ornament on frames, altarpieces and other objects were described by Cennini in the 15th century and how the practice became more general and more sophisticated in the last quarter of the 18th century in France and spread elsewhere, since Paris was the centre of fashion and excellence. These methods are still used by the dwindling number of bespoke framemakers today in many countries.

There is a widespread misunderstanding among picture dealers, antique dealers and collectors about cast frames. Each being equal in design and appearance, a carved frame is more desirable, but not all that much. In any case, each is very rarely equal in design. In museums and national collections carved and cast frames hang together and very few people can tell the difference. The main reason that many antique dealers rate cast frames lower is that they have some difficulty repairing them. Either they cannot get the skilled labour or do not want the expense or trouble; probably a mixture of both. I hope to show in a later chapter how anyone with ten intelligent fingers can restore many frames from a few fragments adhering to the wood. The only question is to what extent it is worth while.

The search for frames from which moulds can be taken is a chore. They can be borrowed from friends, a process that takes time after the word has got out that they are needed. Old and severely damaged frames can be bought cheaply. It is a mystery to me why people try to sell them, since without the expertize and labour they are valueless.

Deals can be done with dealers. A loan of a frame in return for repairing some less damaged frames. Given the initiative, old frames begin to appear, but not all are suitable. Avoid large neo-rococo or swept frames at first, or indeed mouldings that are not pleasing to the eye. Most will be 19th-century frames, some of which were superb, particularly those which, under the influence of Ruskin, echo Renaissance designs or classical (i.e. early 17th-century) motifs. Gothic frames inspired by Pugin and Viollet le Duc sometimes appear. The more you learn about ornament evolution and fashion the better. Only frames finished in burnished water gilding, as bright and shining as an Inca treasure, should be avoided, for fear of harming the extremely delicate leaf, but these are very rare indeed. In the whole of the Tate Gallery in London I am aware of only one. Otherwise, with old battered oil gilding, or heavily ormolu varnished gilt, no harm is done and, indeed, the frame will lose generations of polluted fallout. Donors can be reassured on this point. As an act of courtesy I usually do odd small repairs and a refreshening of the gilded highlights before returning a borrowed frame, and people seem very happy, as indeed they should be.

Opposite above: The smaller frame is adapted from the design motif of a Japanese sword handle. The larger is cast from the longer side of an Italian baroque frame, two moulds being taken, of the inner and outer mouldings. Here they are used together as in the original, but they can be used separately

Opposite below: The frame on top was cast as usual from the longer side of an existing frame. Art deco frames are rare, since very minimal Bauhaus framing was more common at the time (1930)

The frame beneath is modelled on a Vienna Secession frame and copied from a 1905 catalogue. It is an approximation of a Gustav Klimpt frame

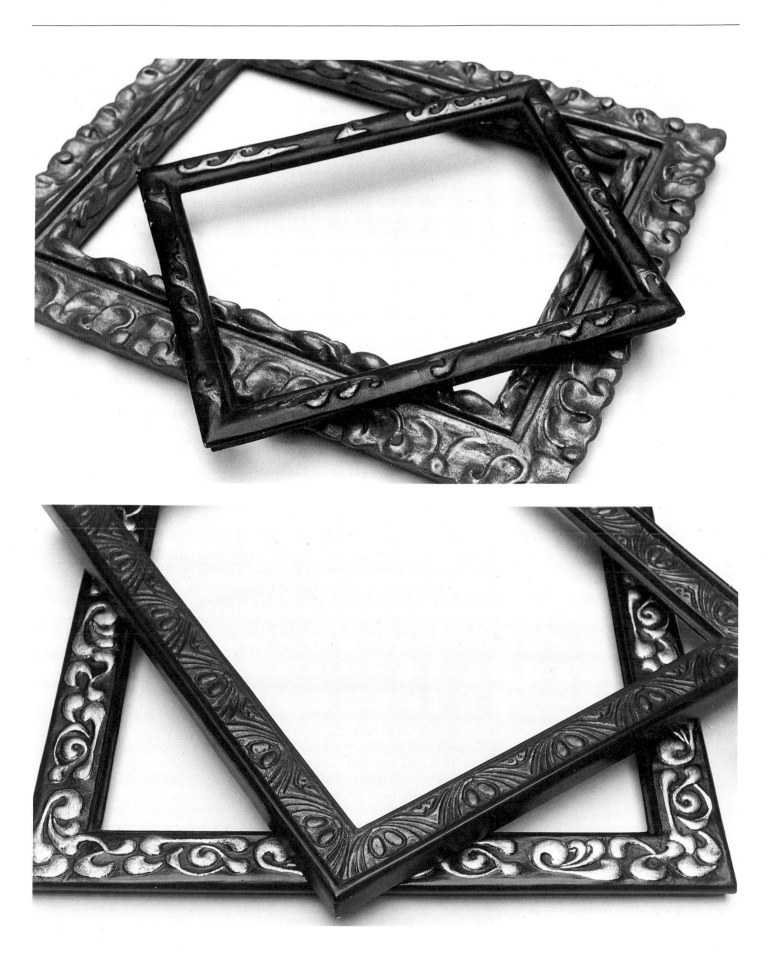

two-thirds full with cold water and gently shake in some measures of Crystacal with the help of a small tin can (tomato purée cans are useful for this) until the water nearly reaches the top. Leave it to stand until the air bubbles stop and carefully pour off the milky water until a white sludge remains (looking like a wet meringue). Pour the watery top into a plastic bucket and *never* down a plughole, since this thin whey will wreck any plumbing system. After a day, clear water can be poured off and the residue knocked out into a refuse bin. The sludge in the beaker should be stirred thoroughly with a cheap brush and is now properly proportioned for use. This is the most reliable mixing method, easy, foolproof and automatically ensures its own correct proportions.

Paint the inside of the silicone rubber mould generously with the white sludge. No greasing is necessary but the non-stick silicones tend to reject water and the brush minimizes tiny bubbles and small hollows that might not fill with direct pouring. Now take the beaker in one hand and, using the same brush, paddle out a flow of white sludge along the mould (see illustration). Stop when three-quarters full and, raising the mould and its bed about an inch (25 mm), tap it on the table a few times, shaking out some more tiny bubbles. If insufficient Crystacal has been mixed, make some more, but without delay and pour until the mould is filled nearly to the top. Place the strip of glass on top of it and push it backwards and forwards a couple of times until the shape of the mould opening shows through the glass. This ensures a constant thickness in successive castings. Some of the Crystacal will squeeze out and form stalactites down the side of the bed. Run a finger along this, under the shelving glass, to remove most of it. These accretions can seal the cast to the bed of the mould and if allowed to harden will make the removal of the cast more hazardous. If the silicone mould has been taken directly from a frame, it will be open at either end. These openings must be stopped with a knob of modelling clay or plasticene. If it is a secondary cast, i.e. two short lengths joined together as mentioned earlier, or perhaps widened by the addition of a narrow wooden fillet or any such, the rubber and bandage can go around the ends, blocking them effectively.

Setting time is about 40 minutes and cannot be hurried. Turn the mould and its bed glass downwards. Remove the bed, cracking off any stalactites that remain, peel off the silicone mould carefully and replace it in its bed. If left for about half an hour the cast will come away from the glass, but it can be freed quickly by swamping it with loaded brushes of water. It must be well dry before its next use.

It sometimes happens that a centre band of ornament must be abstracted from the centre of a wide 19th-century frame. Such a strip, 2 inches (51 mm) wide or more, can be used on its own or fixed to a new wooden matrix of wooden strips and mouldings to taste, as in the original or otherwise. A strip of ornament is something to be used at will. It will be impossible to fit shoulder strips down the centre of a frame, so ignore them and take a straight silicone cast, keeping the back as even as possible, brush the area thinly with petroleum jelly first. It will have no edge to give depth to the positive cast, so trim the edges and lay a thin strip of wood of the desired thickness against either edge and glue them down lightly to a smooth board or glass with the silicone reverse mould snugly in the middle as illustrated. Grease the wooden strips, fill the deepened mould, remove the glass

The first step is to paint, and then puddle the Crystacal into the mould

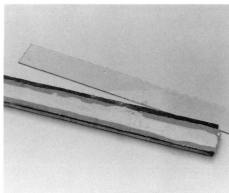

The mould is slightly over-filled. Tap it in order to remove any bubbles

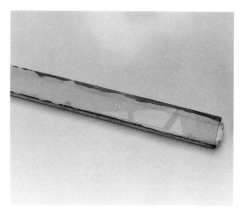

Lay the glass on top and move back and forward to expel any surplus

After setting turn the mould upside down

Remove the cast and the flexible mould from the tray

Gently peel off the mould

The cast remains on the glass, held there by suction

Clean the edges roughly. The cast will come away when dryer or douche with water for speed

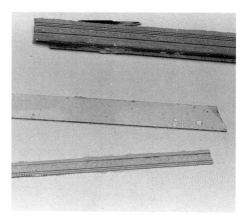

When half-dry the cast can be trimmed with a Surform tool or rasp

when set, prise off the wooden strips and take the cast off the rubber. It will now have a chosen constant thickness. Trim the edges smooth and cast again in silicone rubber. If it seems necessary, tape off the areas of the frame before beginning the process.

Mouldings can be designed or copied from exhibitions unavailable for casting, particularly 'running patterns' (repeated designs). Capacity depends on modelling ability, but useful designs can be copied from drawings or gallery photographs. Part of a Spanish baroque frame is illustrated here, made up from a photograph of old Madrid framers' drawings. This most gracious of frames, dark with sombre soft gold in places, is most flattering to portraits or even rich and more formal abstracts. The second example is a flat, mid-19th-century Gothic frame adapted from one in the Scottish National Gallery, Edinburgh. Both were reconstructed similarly, with modelling clay on a flat board. The centre and corner ornaments of the Spanish frame were straightforward, the rubber mould being taken directly from the greased clay. The outer and inner border, characteristic of this type of frame, consist of repeated units. One of each was modelled and cast in silicone rubber. From time to time, over nearly a week, a cast was taken from each mould in quick-setting dental plaster. These were sandpapered clean and struck down at short intervals on a strip of wood, against a straight-edge. The two lines of motifs were then cast in silicone rubber.

The Gothic frame, shown here in rather extreme use, was reconstructed from the main features of a frame on display. Since it exactly suited a series of small dark mid-19th-century landscapes brought by students, I decided that a copy would be useful in a variety of ways. The flat frame was quattrocento in style, a flat with an inner and outer moulding with a running pattern of gilt Gothic 'stonework'. One unit of this double ogee tracery was drawn, carefully centred so that it could be accurately joined to cast duplicates and cut out in mounting board. The clay was modelled on this and cast in silicone rubber. Casts were taken from this in quick-setting dental plaster and joined together, glued to a board and tidied up. A silicone mould was then taken of the assembly and set in a bed as described earlier. Frail to handle when cast, it became strong when glued to the wooden flat of the moulding.

Both these designs are soft in contour and easy to model. More detailed units of pattern should first be modelled and cast in plaster. Make a little clay wall around the unit and pour in dental plaster in a thin creamy state, always adding plaster to water and pouring off the surplus 'whey'. Tap to remove air bubbles. The reverse shape can then be crisped with small tools, sharpened small screwdrivers, chisels made by hammering the end of nails, filing and sharpening. Squeezes can then be taken from the oiled mould with clay, and mounted on a board and reproduced as earlier. If the pull is difficult to extract (its back must be smooth), fill the mould with an epoxy putty and chip away the mould when the cast has hardened, not forgetting to grease it first. A variety of Renaissance patterns, undulates, grecos and so on, can be produced in this way. Irregular shapes can be reversed by first modelling and casting and then making a paper template of the cast and turning it upside down to get the exact outline for the reverse.

Any intelligent framer can extend this technology as needs demand given a reasonable knowledge of art history or reference books.

Far left: A frame from the neo-baroque second empire

Left: Chinese corner ornaments, adapted from a Museum exhibit

Below, from left to right: Variegated colours in gesso; Persian tile pattern; undulating renaissance bronze; undulating renaissance in gilt; Chinese moulding in green jade glaze; imitation tortoise shell; Chinese cartouch

Museums are a prime source. The Chinese frame (see illustration) was taken from a bronze Ming ritual vessel (1368–1643), a unit of the repeating design being copied in a sketchbook. This unit was modelled in clay, although wax can also be used. Crisp detail was avoided in the clay and the piece resembled a tile in low relief 1×6 inches (25×150 mm). A silicone mould was made of this and half-a-dozen plaster casts taken. These were carefully stuck to a strip of glass and the pattern smoothed and sharpened by carving. The joints were patched with soft plaster and the background cross-hatched with an awl and a sliding setsquare, a technique used on gesso on neo-rococo 19th-century frames.

Many basic designs are common to a wide range of cultures: a Greek key pattern can be found in Korean and Japanese design and I have seen and used a Papuan bark cloth design which is pure Jugen-stil-Klimt. The finished pattern was then cast in silicone rubber and the resulting frames were finished in a lustrous green transparent glaze to resemble jade or a celadon pottery glaze. Much later I discovered some similar Chinese frames in the Lever Museum, Port Sunlight.

When taking a silicone rubber mould from a corner or centre ornament on a baroque or rococo frame, two successive moulds should be made if the intention is for permanent use rather than a passing repair. If a clay squeeze is taken from the first mould it can be flattened onto a sheet of glass and trimmed, tidied and sharpened, particularly when the clay has dried 'cheese' hard. Lightly oil the mould before taking the squeeze and hold the clay briefly under a cold tap after 'squeezing' it, to wash off some of the oil. Corner and centre ornaments cannot usually be cast in Crystacal, which is rigid. The cast must be flexible when wet to accommodate itself to the slope and curve of a particular frame, and must be pressed or squeezed from the silicone rubber mould in a dough-like gesso composition or paste, which will be described in the section dealing with the repair of old frames, or making parts of certain ornamented ones.

Driven by necessity I had to devise a means for casting designs onto wood in cold poured metals. These are used widely in sculpture and examples are to be seen in most mixed exhibitions, though not usually recognised as such. Cold poured metal sculpture is made of a heavy veneer of metal over fibre glass and polyester resin which polishes, burnishes or can be patinated like a hot poured casting, though the process is much cheaper and can be done by the artist without sending the work to a foundry. The most common metals, in the form of very fine powders, are bronze, brass, nickel, aluminium and copper. A mixture of aluminium and nickel with a touch of brass gives a reasonable silver. The finished objects can be left to gather their own natural discolouration, but for framing, the use of a metal polish every six months or so seems to look better, unless the frame is built in vast proportions.

Adapted to cast mouldings for frames or even furniture, the appearance is unusual, but sufficiently conventional, metal being what it is, as to be reassuringly acceptable. The most outstanding metal frame known to me is a broad flat frame in copper, designed by Holman Hunt for his 'May Morning on Magdalen Tower' in the Lever Gallery, Port Sunlight. Its symbols of Spring, fish, clouds and frogs in low relief strangely do not intrude on the painting, proving that you can break every alleged rule in the book if you know how.

Cold metal castings can be taken from almost any silicone mould of a section of frame moulding already described and bonded on strips of wood. These adapt to a frame moulding in a variety of proportions.

There are specialized books on cold casting in sculpture but, briefly, a suitable amount of polyester resin is activated with its hardener in a small PVC cup (sawn-off detergent container), enough to cover the area in a generous coat. Three or four drops of hardener should be enough. Mix thoroughly and trickle in enough of the special fine metal powder to achieve a thin paste. This is painted onto the mould and allowed to harden (one hour in a warm room, less in hot sunshine). Now mix enough resin and hardener to generously fill the mould nearly level, and add any of the inert filler powders supplied, slate, barytes, chalk, to make a liquid dough, and fill the mould. Carefully set a strip of wood of exactly the same width as the mould on top of the grey goo and press it gently to settle level with the top of the mould. Its edges must be aligned carefully along the edges of the mould. This will take a little longer to set, but the squeezed surplus will indicate when. Peel off the silicone mould and trim the edge surplus with a sharp knife. It will not look very attractive at first until a thin film of resin is scrubbed off with fine steel wool, when the metal will be revealed. The steel wool, however fine, leaves a slightly scored surface and benefits from buffing on a cloth wheel with rouge. Such wheels are available for attachment to electric drills, clamped in a stand, well-known to home handymen. After such a burnishing, it is necessary to clean the surface with the type of metal polish made up into a cotton swab. This removes the rouge embedded in deep undercuts. Do not bother to scour out every little hollow from the beginning of this process. The unpolished hollows add depth by contrast with the metal gleam of the highlights.

It might well be necessary to set a band of metal ornament along the centre of a moulding, necessarily a flat section. In such a case cut a strip of mounting board or a very thin strip of wood and bond this to the casting as just described. Either of these can be handled easily and bonded anywhere with a contact adhesive. If mounting board is used, lay the cast between two pieces of board with a weight, since it tends to curl when curing, which goes on for a few days after it has set.

Polyester resin can be used to produce a very convincing ivory. The prepared resin should be whitened by the addition of titanium oxide pigment and a pinch of yellow ochre pigment and used as a first coat like the metal powder mixture. When the cast has set it should be rubbed with steel wool to expose the colour. It can either be waxed and polished or stained with a very thin umber wash in thin size, rubbed almost clean with a damp cloth and then waxed.

Tortoise, or more properly turtle shell, has been used for ornament in furniture and in some Dutch wave pattern frames, popular in the 17th century. For repairs, a convincing effect can be made by treating a piece of glass with wax and resin-parting lacquer. Paint the glass with resin, faintly tinted with dry pigment yellow ochre, broken in patches by a darker tint and perhaps shaded with a little burnt umber pigment. Streak this with some opaque burnt umber mixed in resin with thinner and translucent added. It is essential to copy from a piece of polished shell, a hand mirror, brush or whatever. Finish off with a couple of coats of clear resin and it can be prised off the glass when set. Sometimes the original shell was set over silver leaf to enhance the translucency.

GESSO, FINISHES AND GILDING

GESSO

IF YOU SCRATCH any ornamental frame, simple or ornate, cast or carved, a layer of red clay will show beneath the old gilt and a thicker layer of white below that again. The latter is liquid gesso, *gesso sottile* (It.) or sometimes in English 'pencil white'. Its purpose is to form a manageable foundation to give a desired texture, smooth, polished or deliberately roughened or textured. The Egyptians used something like it and Cennini's formula written in the 1470s is virtually the same as the one that I describe below. Up to the 16th century it was the universal ground for paintings and is still used on wooden panels. It can consist of little more than powdered chalk (whiting) and glue size, but this is liable to cracking and has a gritty texture, and needs a further refinement.

The addition of some 'slaked' or deadened plaster of Paris makes a critical difference in the behaviour of the liquid gesso. It is made in the following manner from dental plaster for ease and quality. Add a tablespoonful (15 ml) of dental plaster to its own bulk in water. Do not stir, but pour off the watery liquid on top, but not into a drain. Stir and pour the thick cream onto a newspaper and time its setting which will take about 20 minutes. Fill a bucket three-quarters full of water and trickle in about two cupfuls of dental plaster. It is now necessary to stir the thin mixture for more than the setting time of the plaster, perhaps half an hour. Vigorous stirring is not needed. Indeed one can read or do nearby chores, stirring with a stick every minute or so, so as to keep the water white. The plaster tends to sink to the bottom and harden, or half harden, and this must be prevented. Then leave it for several hours and pour or syphon off the clear water on top.

If, after this, it is possible to pour the white cream into narrower jars (preserving jars can be used), the process will continue, but it is easier to pour off two inches (50 mm) of water from a jar than $\frac{1}{4}$ inch (6 mm) of water from a bucket. Eventually a thicker white mud will precipitate, which can be used. Seal the jar to prevent its drying completely. This white mud consists of tiny crystalline particles which make a durable aggregate with the coarser particles of chalk, causing the gesso to paint on creamily and resist cracking or flaking, its two besetting sins.

To assemble the ingredients of the liquid gesso, prepare some size as before, with four tsp (20 ml) to the quarter pint (150 ml) of water and melt in hot water. Put (let us say) two tbsp (30 ml) of gilders whiting (chalk) in a bowl, and one dessertspoon (7 ml) of slaked plaster: 1 to 4. Mix and carefully spill in some hot size, stirring each time. Stop when it is a thick cream. If you add too much size, add more whiting and slaked plaster.

'Monna Vanna' by Dante Gabriel Rossetti.
The frame faintly suggests a renaissance
structure because of the ornamented flats
but it is untypical of Rosetti's more
characteristic and original frame designs

Above, clockwise from top left: Northern Renaissance 'Tudor' frame; Neo Rococo with transparent black glaze; Indian painting ornamental ogee frame with grey blue and silver highlights; mid-19th-century gothic frame; gilt on Indian Red; the first and last are from sketches and the remainder are cast from originals

Right: Coloured glazes in polyester resin

Left: Mottling, stippling and sponging on gesso (George Brandreth)

Flake some unbleached beeswax the volume of a walnut into a clean can and add about a quarter of that volume of carnauba wax, flaked off with a penknife into a customary brittle powder. Slightly more than cover the wax mixture with white spirit (naphtha or mineral spirit or turps substitute). Place on a gentle hotplate or very low gas ring covered with wire mesh and melt to complete dissolution, which takes a few minutes. Have a square of warmed glass ready, and make a pyramid of burnishing bronze with a dent in the top, having mixed two different tones of gold to taste if necessary. This can be modified later. The can of wax will be hot, so hold it with pliers and pour some wax into the crater. Work this with a palette knife or a flexible kitchen knife until a smooth thick paste results, adding more wax or powder to achieve this end. Do not spare the palette knifing to get a homogeneous mass. Smear a fingertipful on black newsprint headlines and if these are obliterated scoop the mass into a small airsealed jar.

Airsealing is important to avoid evaporation. Seal the jar in a small freezer bag for extra safety, and it will keep indefinitely. If it dries too hard for easy application, scrape it onto a warm piece of glass and work in a few drops of white spirit with a knife and reseal. To make a useful silver amalgam, use aluminium powder with a little pale-gold bronze powder added, to taste. Silver is warmer in tone than most people realize. In mixing the paste the point to stop adding powder is reached just before it becomes friable or crumbly. The aim is to get in as much metal as possible without drying the paste. If the paste does become too friable, then add a fraction more wax and work in until satisfied.

To apply the amalgam, use the pad of the forefinger which is warm and subtle. Do not lift a lump or gobbet, just a thick coating on the finger pad. Work this onto all the prepared surface as firmly as possible, concentrating at first on the highlights. The finger is best, but for odd corners, hollows and ridges, a cheap small hog or similar brush, cut down to $\frac{1}{4}$ inch (6 mm) can be used. After about an hour in a warm room, the white spirit will evaporate. The longer it is left the better; then it can be vigorously polished, preferably with a 3-inch (75-mm) square of woolly sheepskin or a traditional soft yellow cotton duster. After some days the highlights can be burnished with an agate tool.

Antiqueing

Many, if not most, ornamented frames look better and serve brightly coloured paintings better if they are antiqued. There are various ways of doing this, but with wax gilding the simplest is to use a less reactive colour than red for the bole coat over the gesso: warm brown to burnt umber is a useful colour scale. Use as previously directed and apply the wax amalgam over the highlights only. Apply lightly and evenly with gentle strokes of the finger pad, and avoid a heavy smear which is almost impossible to remove. After several hours, polish as described earlier. The hollows and crevices will remain dark brown, like centuries of smoky accretion. If they are too violent in dark contrast, stipple on a little gold with the previously described cut-down brush, after partly exhausting its charge on a piece of newspaper.

As mentioned earlier, if an entirely gold surface is needed, as for a mirror glass, flood on a coat of burnishing bronze in size after

Opposite: A selection of mouldings dating from the Renaissance to present day, including a Chinese and a Persian example

Baroque and rococo mouldings are not
formed from simple repeating patterns and
cannot be mitred just anywhere. To decrease
a length, remove a suitable unit of design,
possibly two, and rejoin the rest. To
lengthen, cut the design and insert newly
cast units and tidy up

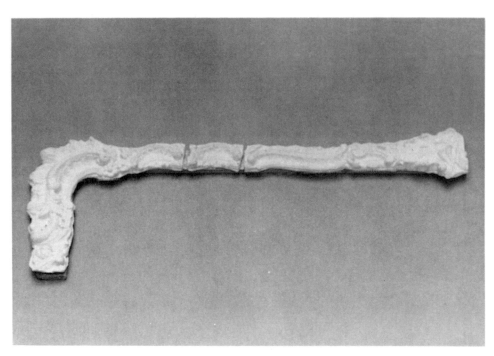

design, the structure of a C scroll or acanthus leaf, and make a line
drawing of its curves and symmetries. It need not be an accomplished
drawing, merely a guide to structure which will make the modelling
easier. Sometimes this modelling can be done on the broken area of
frame, using a couple of nail pins to support it if necessary.

If it is very extensive, cast the sound area in alginate or silicone
rubber, take a clay 'squeeze' of the right thickness, lay it flat on a
board and the new area can be fashioned on to it with greater ease.
Remould the clay entirely in silicone rubber and not only will it
enable the frame to be repaired but it can be kept for further use in
refabricating injured frames of a similar kind and for making new
ones. This has been mentioned before in a different context, but is
worth repeating more specifically.

There are a few points to remember when taking a cast from a
sound section of a frame to replace a missing or badly damaged section. Always make the flexible mould from an area of design slightly
larger than the one you wish to replace. Clear the missing or broken
area to some logical point in the pattern. Do not try to subdivide a
flower cluster or a piece of fussy strapwork, but chisel it off the wood,
leaving space for a coherent area of design as self-sufficient as possible. Only common sense can decide. Before taking a 'squeeze' in
gesso pasta or composition make a 'squeeze' in modelling clay or
warm plasticene and lay it near you as a reference to the design
pattern, which is sometimes difficult to 'read' in reverse in the mould
with any accuracy. An eye judgment can then be made as to where to
trim the gesso pasta insert so that it fits in snugly, joining on to where
it should. Lay the gesso 'squeeze' on the table and cut it to size with a
sharp thin knife. Make sure it is the right thickness, which is apparent if it is laid in place temporarily. If not, take a second squeeze.
Often the same lump of gesso pasta can be used, but dunk it again into
the size and reroll it between the hands.

MAKING ANTIQUE FRAMES FROM DRAWINGS OR PHOTOGRAPHS

FOR THOSE WITH any facility in modelling, any running patterns can be copied. Most ornamented mouldings consist of single unit of pattern, perhaps 3 or 4 inches (75–100 mm) long, repeated indefinitely. No particular attempt is usually made to align a pattern at a corner, as when hanging wall paper, since this might well involve cutting the sides too long or too short.

When making home-made decorated mouldings, ingenuity can be used to fudge certain ornate patterns by a little subtraction from the pattern on one side with a small chisel and a little rebuilding on the other side of the corner with epoxy putty or gesso pasta. This can be rubbed down and sharpened on drying so that the pattern appears to run around the corner on the finished frame, but in fact does not.

In ornament, the eye is more easily deceived than with austere mouldings or parallel ridges and spooned sections. Alternatively, a suitable corner ornament can be added whenever the design allows. Sometimes this is not desirable, since certain paintings demand a rectangular profile, and corner ornaments themselves vary so much in opulence and relative simplicity that care in choice is needed. Sometimes a small corner ornament can be used on a frame not extending beyond its outer profile. Roundel ornaments which can sometimes be taken from old pieces of furniture were sometimes used in the 19th century and earlier. These, as the name suggests, are

This flowing pattern meets uneasily at the corners. By cutting away and building up with gesso paste, polyfilla or epoxy putty, a continuous mitreless flow results

Previous Pages.
Left (*underneath*): A Spanish Baroque frame;
(*on top*) An art deco frame with doctored
corners

Right: A copy of a Nicholas Hilliard
(*c.* 1547–1619) miniature in enamel on copper.
The rather spiky strapwork frame was
common in northern Europe in Tudor times

round ornaments rather like carved draughtsmen or rosettes. Dante Gabriel Rossetti designed several with his private esoteric symbols for some of his frames. Corner ornaments which derive from the baroque and the rococo styles were not devised to cover an untidy corner, but they certainly have that effect in practice.

The example I have chosen for producing a frame from drawings, line sketches taken in a gallery, or from photographs is Spanish baroque. My reasons are threefold. It is a gracious type of frame, like much else in Spanish design, austere yet sensual. The fine elements to which I have reduced it are simple to model with no intricacy of C scrolls or artificial foliage, and it is an extremely usable design for portraits and much else and would be more widely used if it were more readily available. It is rare to find one in antique galleries or auctions and they are not very common in public collections either. Even in the Rastro flea market in Madrid where they could once be seen now and then, they have virtually disappeared, probably into dealers' stocks.

All Spanish baroque frames are slightly different. A style of frame is not like a model of a car, where each one is identical. What they share is a style, a proportion and a common rhythm of ornament. Gothic cathedrals are very different from each other, but they share common recognizable qualities. Art Deco cinema design, now being reappraised, varied from high street to high street, but there was a common style, recognizable from the top of a bus in a snowstorm. So it is with frames in a given style. The example given here has been shorn of certain exuberances, but not very much, and this is quite allowable.

Like most baroque frames, there are emphatic corner ornaments and centre ornaments and a running (repeated) inner and outer border. Sometimes one or the other of these border strips is wider or a little more elaborate, but not much and not always. I am concerned here with shapes that can be formed easily. Anyone who can, is welcome to elaborate. The illustration shows a couple of working sketches

A corner adjusted by modelling a continuous flow of ornament

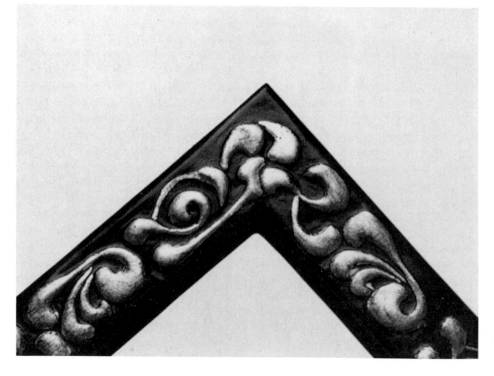

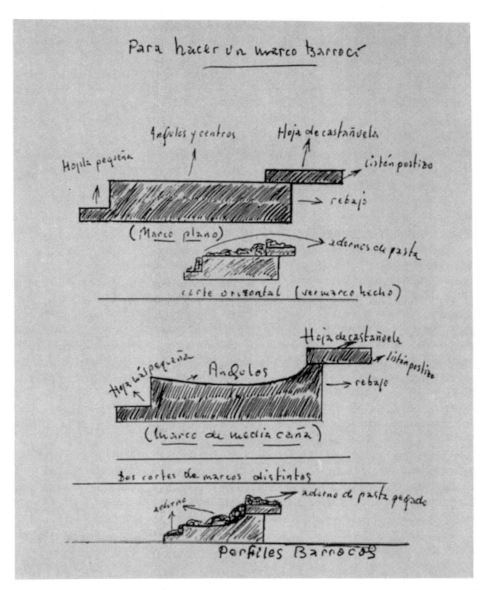

Left: A sheet of framers' sketches from Madrid by an old and honourable framer Eugenio Garcia Harranz. Classical ornament, however curvasious, was based on material form, abstracted and ornamented. The first drawing below is a natural vine. The bottom drawing is 'artificial'. Most 'artificial' derivations are more difficult to recognize

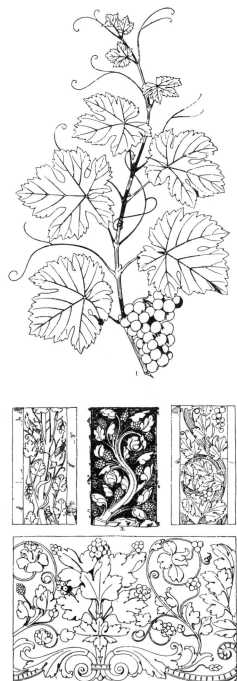

from an old Spanish framing atelier, the sort of rough note used by framers for centuries, sometimes scribbled by the artist. Examples by Rembrandt and Constable exist. Thousands must have been used to light pipes or stoves. These show the slightly variable profiles of Spanish baroque and the proportions can be modified to taste.

Few shapes are simpler to assemble: it is just three strips of wood glued together, all flat, to which ornament is added. This consists of four corner ornaments, which in this Italian-style frame do not break the rectangular outer profile. There are two centre ornaments of different sizes, one for the short sides and one for the longer; it is not essential to have both, although together they allow finer control of visual weight; by using only the smaller one a smaller, uncrowded frame can be made. Quite a lot of the surface of a Spanish baroque frame is plain, usually of a dark colour. The outer and inner wooden strips, one forming the rebate, are decorated with a running strip of abstract repeated ornament, both simple but different. I will deal with these first.

Both consist of a repeated motif, one of two modified rectangles

Various frame ornaments, including baroque, rococo and classical

A glazed frame with gold intaglio tiles to echo a Mogul painting

Top: A Spanish baroque assembling pattern for an outer border, made with casts from silicone mould of original clay model

Centre: A similar assembling of an inner border

Bottom: The metamorphosis of a unit shape from a piece of modelling clay

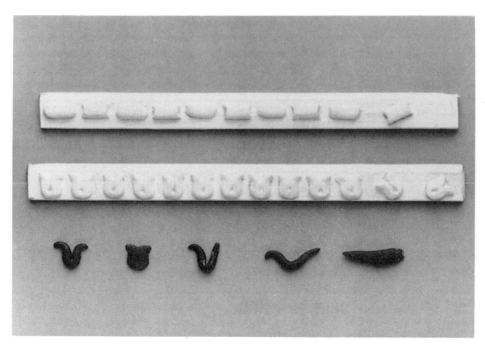

A silicone rubber mould of the outer and inner borders of the moulding

and the other a keyhole or omega shape, as shown. Shape the two-rectangle unit in clay on a piece of glass to a chosen size: stick two strips of masking tape the required width apart and exactly parallel on the back of the glass. Model the clay shapes on the top side, guided by the tapes. Form a small silicone mould from the two rectangles, which are treated as one unit. Model the omega shape on glass from a worm of clay, tapering at both ends, and bend and mould it on the glass. Two or three tries may be necessary to get a tapering worm of the right length. The edges must be at an angle of 90° or slightly less, to the glass base to avoid undercuts. With a rubber mould a degree of undercutting is allowable, but in this case it is not necessary. A crisp edge in any modelling gives a greater illusion of hollowness or undercutting. This is then cast in silicone rubber, at the same time as the first. It is easier and more economic to cast several units at the same time.

This part of the job can be done at odd moments over several days. These units are then cleaned and rubber cemented onto glass along a taped-down strip of wood used as a straight-edge which is removed on completion. The strips are best formed up to about 3 feet (1 m) long, convenient for storing in a cupboard, the ultimate criterion. It is quicker to use the more rapid-setting dental plaster for such casting since it halves the waiting time, and no great hardness is needed for the pattern. A silicone rubber mould is made of these casts, just as if they were part of a frame moulding.

The very abstract designs of the corner and centre ornaments derive from a vegetable pattern. Much of Greco Roman architectural design was semi-abstracted from natural leaves, acanthus, laurel, ivy and so forth, originally symbols of gods: ivy for Dionysius, laurel for Apollo. These became increasingly conventionalized so that an 'artificial' leaf became in architects' or framers' parlance an exact formal thing.

Examples of this are very useful when analyzing frame mouldings. By the late 17th century the full flowering of baroque led to wild and, it must be said, agreeable abstraction. It is difficult at times to recognize the interlaced strapwork on a Louis IV frame as rarefied foliage.

The corner and centre ornaments on Spanish baroque frames vary greatly but all are recognizable as such. They must be of the same width throughout and this can be done by modelling them on glass with parellel bands of tape on the under side, as a guide. It is safer, however, to draw out the general structure of the design on mount board and cut out the pieces with a knife or scissors. Cement these onto glass or smooth hardboard and model on top of them. When drawing, a simple black outline of the main masses is enough and a pair of compasses or dividers ensures the balanced dimensions of similar shapes facing in two different directions. It is not a lengthy job and is closer to pattern making than what is normally considered modelling. Make two or three silicone rubber moulds of the pieces and they are ready to use.

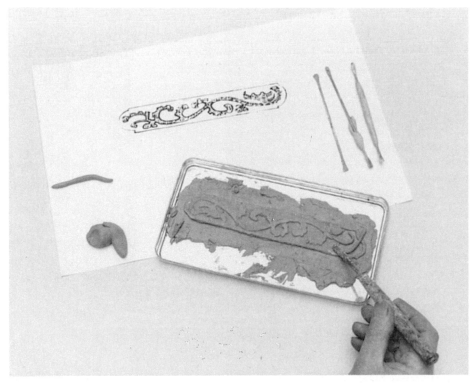

A Chinese cartouche ornament modelled in clay from a drawn pattern using hand-made spatulas

Far left: A Renaissance pattern resembling a Persian border, and used for a mogul painting

The pattern from a Chinese urn finished like ivory. The mount is in raw silk

A Neo-gothic moulding adapted from a frame in the National Gallery, Edinburgh

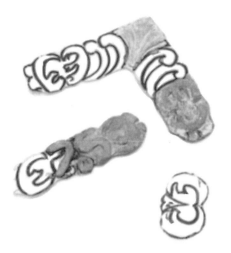

Above: A Spanish baroque modelling ornament in clay on a pattern drawn on thick card

Below: A silicone rubber mould

Casts in Crystacal

In this sort of modelling I find that the spatulas available in art shops are not convenient, being more suitable for larger heads, figures or whatever. Some can be pared thinner to give a more blade-like effect, which is the most useful. There is more paring, scraping and 'carving' than usual and the desired result must be smooth and crisp.

Tools can be made from nails and pieces of thick wire (such as old coat hangers). Cut the head from a 4-inch (100-mm) nail and heat one end red hot. As quickly as possible, beat it with a hammer until about $\frac{1}{2}$–$\frac{3}{4}$ inches (12–19 mm) of it broadens out to a spade, this does not take long. Hammer until the 'blade' is a little thicker than needed and then file it to a rounded paddle shape and smooth both sides, finishing them off with emery paper. Six inches (150 mm) of heavy gauge wire will make a double-ended tool of different sized 'blades' or one with a flat chisel-like tip, useful for clearing surfaces. Steel-wool the metal to a fine polish and roughen the shanks with a file. A thickening of epoxy putty or plastic wood will make a handle or grip for the fingers, useful when twirling and turning the spatula when working the clay, plasticene or wax. After modelling, a square hog brush, dipped in water, is useful for smoothing out the surface. It becomes a useful tool for cleaning out hollows where unwanted clay rubble tends to collect. When wet, the highlights can be rubbed smooth with the forefinger. This is usually frowned on in more conventional modelling, but we are dealing here with very elaborate pattern making.

A set of such tools can be made in less than an afternoon, apart from the drying time for the plastic wood or epoxy putty, but they will last a lifetime, though they are readily stolen and easily lost.

While it has nothing to do with the immediate subject, such tools, shaped to whim and experience, are useful for modelling medallions, medals and the like, which indeed can occur on specially designed frames. In lighter moments with students, we have designed frames with dogs' heads, cats' heads, human portraits and Chinese dragons as corner ornaments for frame follies, often for unusual mirror glass frames, and they never fail to stimulate conversation and give pleasure. It is not uncommon to have to copy or forge an eagle or a crest of some sort on a mirror glass frame. If the mass of the modelling looks like being too heavy, coat the inside of the mould with Crystacal $\frac{1}{4}$ inch (6 mm) thick with a brush, and when partly set, lay in strips of medium or coarse jute scrim (not the cotton stuff like bandage) and paint some more Crystacal through the scrim to cement it into the structure, overlapping it slightly.

Two short rods (sawn-off nails) can be incorporated into the casting or dowelled in later, at its base, to slot into a block fixed behind the frame. Fibrous casts can be both strong and light.

Only the narrow outer and inner borders of the Spanish baroque frame are 'running' or repeated units of the same pattern. The corners and centre designs are discontinuous with plain areas between.

The Gothic frame illustrated here was adapted from a frame in the Scottish National Gallery, Edinburgh. Gothic revival was very popular in the mid-19th century, exemplified by Pugin's decorative additions to the Westminster Houses of Parliament or in France by the mediaeval recreations of Viollet le Duc. The phrase may have been originally an expression of the Oxford Movement, or more probably the last kick of the Romantic epoch when Ivanhoe was a world hero from Milan to Boston.

Some Gothic frames were very spiky, with fretted finials and crockets resembling the skyline of Lincoln Cathedral. The Edinburgh frame was quattrocento in its simplicity: a broad central flat with a plain narrow outer and inner border with a repeated double ogee design in relief along the central flat. The copy or adaptation described was devised to frame some small landscapes, dark and mysterious, which seemed suitable for hanging in Schloss Frankenstein.

The flat frame was quattrocento in style, one unit of this double ogee tracery was drawn, carefully centred so that it could be accurately joined to cast duplicates and cut out in mounting board. The clay was modelled on this and cast in silicone rubber. Casts were taken from this in quick-setting dental plaster and joined together, glued to a board and tidied up. A silicone mould was then taken of the assembly and set in a bed as described earlier. Frail to handle when cast, it became strong when glued to the wooden flat of the moulding.

Such designs are soft in contour and easy to model. More detailed units of pattern should first be modelled and cast in plaster. Make a little clay wall around the unit and pour in dental plaster in a thin creamy state, always adding plaster to water and pouring off the surplus 'whey'. Tap to remove air bubbles. The reverse shape can then be crispened with small tools, sharpened small screwdrivers, chisels made by hammering the end of nails, filing and sharpening. A squeeze can then be taken from the oiled mould with clay, and mounted on a board and reproduced as earlier. If the pull is difficult to extract (its back must be smooth), fill the mould with an epoxy putty and chip away the mould when the cast has hardened, not forgetting to grease it first. A variety of Renaissance patterns, undulates, grecos etc., can be contrived in this way. Irregular shapes can be reversed by first modelling and casting and then making a paper template of the cast and turning it upside down to get the exact outline for the reverse.

Any inventive framer can extend this technology as needs demand given, as should be, a reasonable knowledge of art history or books of reference. Museums are a prime source. The Chinese frame was taken from a bronze Ming ritual vessel (1368–1643), a unit of the repeating design being copied in a sketchbook by the showcase and redrawn to actual scale in line on thin paper. The background was an even ribbon of clay on a board crosshatched with a nail and a set square. A similar ribbon of clay was levelled on a talced board to prevent sticking and the shape marked through the paper outline with a fine ballpoint. It was then cut free from the rest of the clay, with a small knife, tidied up, moistened on the back and laid on the moistened crosshatched ribbon and pressed down. Finer detail was then modelled or carved on the design. A silicone mould was made of this and half a dozen plaster casts taken. These were carefully stuck to a strip of glass and the pattern smoothed and sharpened by carving. The joints were patched with soft plaster and the background crosshatched with an awl and a sliding set-square, a technique used on gesso on neo-rococo 19th-century frames, but accurate in this case.

A silicone rubber mould was then taken of the finished pattern and a transparent green-blue glaze finish using an epoxy resin was used to give an oriental-style appearance.

In the search for 'ethnic' designs for adaptation to a frame moulding the field is wide, depending on one's perspicacity.

An eagle mirror glass crest in hollow reinforced Crystacal, which is light and strong

OVAL, BOX, FLOATING, AND TRAY, LUNETTE GEORGIAN PRINT FRAMES

OVAL FRAMES

VASARI DESIGNED some oval frames for the Medicis in the 16th century, but their popularity increased in the 17th and 18th centuries, usually with a few C scrolls added. Watteau shows them in his shop sign for the dealer Gersaint, and towards the end of the century there was a revival, with neo-classical additions, before the French Revolution. They are rare in English records.

All of these would have been large, 3 or 4 feet (91 or 122 cm) high, carved in sections in wood and joined together. Today large oval frames are used rarely, if at all, by painters, and small ones are made in Italy, cut in wood by an ingenious lathe for the photographic trade, but even this practice is dying out. The vignetted oval photo portraits of the first decades of this century have been replaced by rectangular colour prints.

There are two ways to frame an oval picture of any size, be it in oil on canvas board (canvases on stretchers are rectangular), a wooden panel or anything else.

A spandrelled frame is rectangular with an oval or a round opening. They were in vogue from the latter part of the 18th century to the middle of the 19th century. The outer frame can be made in the manner described earlier, with a fairly narrow moulding. The centre is cut from plywood or hardboard to the correct oval proportion. The painting shown is really a compressed sphere rather than a geometrical oval. The four corners are the spandrels, an architectural term, and were always decorated like a grandfather clock face.

The four spandrel ornaments, typical of this kind of frame, can either be modelled in clay from some reference source and cast in silicone rubber and then Crystacal (it lies on a flat surface), or taken from part of a corner ornament from a rococo frame. Some imaginative ingenuity is called for.

The rebate, which is also the inner border, is a narrow Boule moulding cast in gesso pasta and bent around the curve in sections. A little fudging was needed at the joints. Since the rebate was impossibly shallow, it was deepened from behind with a discontinuous oval of blocks made from pieces of one-by-one (25 × 25 mm) glued on. A variety of mouldings and ornaments, classical, some baroque and more rococo, can be combined in constructing a spandrelled frame of this kind, depending on occasion and opportunity. Access to old frames for taking silicone moulds is naturally important.

A purely oval frame of any size can be 'run' in gesso on a core. 'Running' consists of painting or carefully pouring gesso over a core of wood and pulling over this a template cut in metal. In the first few 'runnings', moving the template over the partly covered core, only

Far right: A copy of a Tudor miniature (enamel on copper) in a spandrelled 19th-century frame. It is a Crystacal cast on wood and gilded larger spandrelled frames have much richer ornament

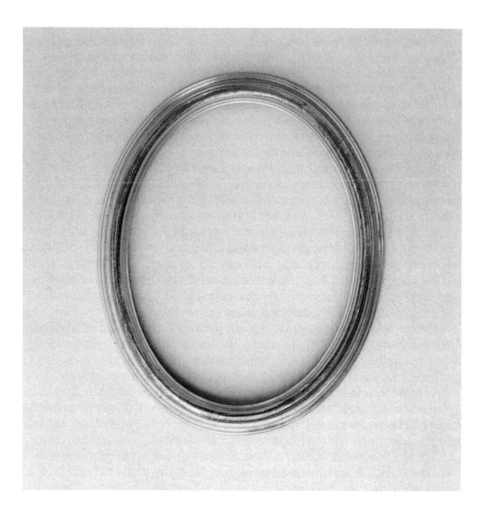

A plain oval frame, used mostly for
photographs from 1890–1918

A small corner ornament gives a simple
stained moulding the feeling of period, as if
from an old country house library

This frame isolates the drawing like a painting hanging on a textured screen or wall. At the same time it fulfils the conventions of framing

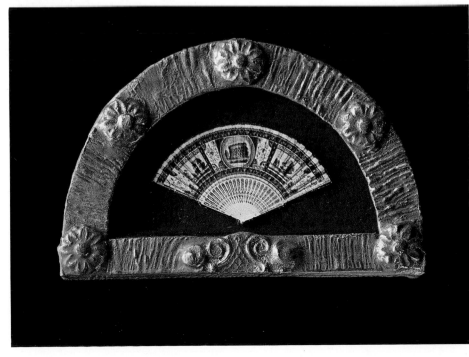

A lunette frame for an 18th-century fan (small model)

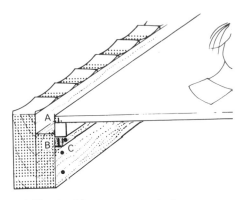

A 'floating' frame serves to isolate a painting. Some Paul Klee paintings have variants of this

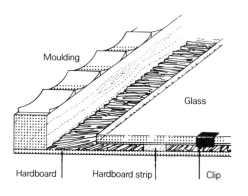

A 'tray' frame gives quiet isolation with emphatic presentation to line drawings etc

FLOATING FRAMES

An effective way to frame certain small canvases, say up to 20 × 30 inches (510 × 750 mm) or thereabouts, is to surround the bare canvas on its stretcher with a shallow trough of darkness which gives an unusual isolation to the painting. The illustrations give an idea of how this can be achieved. The frame should be deep and any ornament should be unemphatic. The purpose is to induce a deep shadow between the canvas edge, which should be dark, and the inside of A, also darkened, shrouding the top of B, also darkened, in a rim of deep shadow.

The wood needed is a matter of choice, but it could consist of two-by-one (50 × 25 mm) (A), 1¼ × 1 inch (30 × 25 mm) (B) and one-by-one (25 × 25 mm) (C). The trough between canvas and A could be covered in dark fabric, but stippled gesso painted with a suitable dark tempera or acrylic colour is probably as good for light absorption and easier to do. The face of the frame is the top of A. A light decorated moulding, ornamented or in wood, can be glued here, but probably textured gesso is enough. With a dark tempera wash, the gesso-textured highlights can be touched with gold or silver amalgam. Quite a number of the paintings of Paul Klee are framed in this way, often with adapted and old ornamented frames. Both he and his heirs had the same finesse of vision that he displayed in his painting.

TRAY FRAMES

An elegant and useful way of framing something light and precious, a drawing, a flat collage or some such, can be done as illustrated. I used it once for a small 17th-century Jesuit map of the canals and ponds of Pekin which had no beginning or end and was far removed from the global or provincial cartography of the time. The frame consists of a narrow moulding which contains a rectangle of hardboard, textured with gesso and colour-washed to taste. This is a chosen size, a kind of mount or matt, larger than the picture. The picture is clipped, with its glass, onto a smaller piece of hardboard and this is glued onto the centre of the frame with its textured backing. The glazed section is raised from its background on two thin strips of wood. The illustrations show the process in cross section. In effect, this frame was made of fairly narrow mouldings with a piece of hardboard cut to fit the rebate.

The picture was trimmed to a rectangle and set on a piece of hardboard of the same size and covered with a piece of glass also of the same size. The trimmed drawing was used to determine the size of the background and the frame that contained it. The larger piece of hardboard was sized and given two coats of gesso. A third coat was combed radially from the centre but the middle area, over which the picture would lie was scraped clean, but not quite as big an area as the picture. Two strips of wood 1 × ¼ inch (25 × 6 mm) and 1 inch (25 mm) shorter than the picture were glued to the background, about an inch (25 mm) in from where the picture would lie. The smaller piece of hardboard was glued in position carefully, on to the two strips and allowed to dry. The picture and glass were then laid on this and fixed with four glass clips, the kind used for unframed but glazed pictures. The purpose of the two 1 × ¼ inch (25 × 6 mm) strips was to raise the picture from the textured background, so that it appeared to 'float', and also to allow space for the glass clips to fit under the smaller piece of hardboard. The degree of isolating texture on the background, the width and nature of the moulding and the general proportions, are matters of judgment and permit many variations, not necessarily similar in general appearance. The example shown has a very light transparent black wash over the background texture, giving a striated grey effect. The effect of some Indian ink greatly thinned with size over a texture is to produce a grey at a distance, but a very lively luminescent grey quite unlike a flat colour. The moulding was in silver, or rather burnished aluminium cast in cold poured resin, and designed and cast to give the effect of a sequence of reflecting highlights, an idea that came from a piece of Bauhaus sculpture. A suitable commercial moulding could have been used.

LUNETTE FRAMES

An object like a painted fan needs to be shown opened, and does not fit easily in a rectangular frame. It is possible, with a little ingenuity, to make a semi-circular or a lunette (less than semicircular) box frame as shown. The degree of ornamentation depends on the fan itself. An 18th-century French fan or an early 19th-century Spanish or Cuban fan can take as much neo-classical or rococo ornament, heavily gilded, as courage allows. East India Company Chinese fans can be either very plain or luxuriously simple in the Chinese manner. The example shown is made from a length of two-by-one (50×25 mm), a strip of hardboard 2 inches (50 mm) deep for the bow. This is usually about one-and-a-half times as long as the straight base but make it one-and-three-quarters for safety. Soak the strip in water for three or four hours until it darkens in colour and bend accurately. Pin one end to the butt of the piece of two-by-one (50×25 mm) and make a suitable curve, then pin the other end to the end of the two-by-one (50×25 mm). The surplus can be sawn off when dry. For safety, wedge a piece of wood from the centre of the straight to the centre of the bow to fit tightly without distortion of the curve. This is removed when the hardboard is dry. Lay the bowed shape on a larger piece of hardboard, mark out its base and cut it out. Pin this to the straight base and fix the bowed part of the base to the bowed strip by cementing a length of 1-inch (25-mm) gauze bandage over the joint, extending $\frac{1}{2}$ inch (12 mm) onto the strip and $\frac{1}{2}$ inch (12 mm) onto the baseboard. It is easier to do this in shorter lengths, 4 to 6 inches (100–150 mm) depending on the curve. Smear contact adhesive on the hardboard, and lay the bandage when still wet. The cement will then penetrate the bandage and bond strongly. In passing, contact adhesives are most easily removed from the finger tips by soaking them in warm water for a minute and then rubbing off the dried cement with a scouring powder. You will now have a bow-shaped box, quite strong, ready for a rebate to fit the glazing.

Glue a strip of $\frac{1}{4} \times \frac{1}{4}$-inch ($6 \times 6$-mm) wood, $\frac{1}{10}$ inch (2·5 mm) down from the top of the straight base, and glue a series of short blocks cut from the same wood to form a discontinuous rebate around the hardboard bow $\frac{1}{10}$ inch (2·5 mm) down from the top. This is the easiest way to get around the curve. Well glued, they will hold firmly. The inside of the box should now be finished off. Glue a second strip of bandage over the inside of the bowed joint to secure it permanently, and tidy up the inside by lining the base and sides up to the rebate in fabric or paper. The fabric on the sides can run up to the top of the rebate, but not on top of it, for the glass must rest there. Since the glazing cannot easily be replaced if broken, it is safer to use one of the available

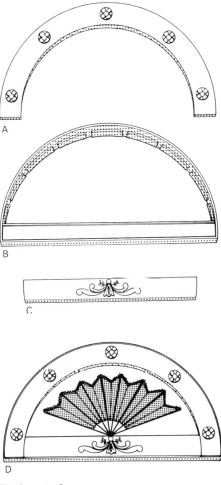

The lunette frame
(A) face of bow
(B) shallow box structure
(C) face of base
(D) assembled parts with gesso, sanding and ornament

transparent plastic sheetings which are cut with a saw and can be trimmed with a file. Care is needed to prevent scratches, always a hazard with plastics, which otherwise have high optical qualities. Any visible part of the rebate strips are better painted black or some dark colour.

At this point fit the fan in place, using looped staples of floral wire, pushed through the baseboard and twisted tightly behind. Lay the glazing in place and give some thought to the finish needed on the face. Using the structure as a measure, draw a curved strip a little over $1\frac{1}{4}$ inches (30 mm) wide and extending across the width of the straight base, that is, extended by 1 inch (25 mm) at either end. A strip of similar width 2 inches (50 mm) shorter than the straight-edge covers the base. Both strips serve to cover the rebate, which is really an upsidedown rebate, and hold the glazing in place, and are cut in hardboard or plywood. Many woodshops will do the cutting for you if you do not have a bandsaw. The plastic glazing should be covered in paper and sticky tape for protection during the finishing.

The hardboard bow facing should be pinned to either end of two-by-one (50×25 mm) base and the straight facing pinned down with three or four pins. The joining along the bowed edge should be secured with a strip of 1-inch (25-mm) gauze bandage, as before, with a contact adhesive. This should be done as smoothly and neatly as possible.

When dry, after a thin coat of size and sufficient coats of gesso to cover the joints and the bandage strips, a last coat can be scratched with a plastic nailbrush, possibly in a radial pattern, and vertically on the sides. After gentle sandpapering the gesso can be coloured opaquely or transparently, touched with wax amalgam, gold or silver. A simple form of ornament of a neo-classical kind can be achieved by making a silicone rubber mould of a rosette, roundel, cameo or even a beautiful button, about 1 inch (25 mm) in diameter, stuck at suitable intervals along the face. It is equally possible, but more arduous, to cast from a suitable silicone rubber mould of a moulding. The straight base can be cast in Crystacal but the curved length must be squeezed in gesso pasta and fixed as previously described. It is even possible to cast and fix some sort of corner ornament at either end of the base and a centre ornament in the centre of the bow.

With luck, fractions of larger ornaments can be squeezed from silicone rubber moulds to suit various needs and to give a suitable period effect. A Chinese bowed frame might be either left fairly plain or decorated with roundels as above, abstracted from a Chinese button, piece of jade or whatever is available. When the surfaces have been gessoed white, they can be glazed a pale green with polyester resin, suggesting jade, or Chinese blue, with a lot of white showing.

GEORGIAN PRINT FRAMES

One of the commonest categories in framing consists largely of prints, engravings, woodcuts, maps and the like, from the late 17th century to the middle of the 19th century. Sadly, these are often cut from old books, but the earlier Italian engravings of classical subjects were often issued in loose folios; Piranesi prints or prints of statues from Herculaneum.

Although modern styles of mounting and framing can be devised effectively, the necessarily simple framing benefits from a period touch, as if the print had hung well-preserved for generations on the study wall of an old country house.

Something of this effect can be achieved easily by choosing a deep ivory mount (or matt), even though this might not have been used in the 1780s. The moulding for the frame should be a 1-inch (25-mm) scooped moulding in white wood, easily available, unfinished, in woodshops. Naturally, oak or anything similar will do as well.

Cut and assemble the frame and stain it with a spirit dye to a dark brown if suitable. Sometimes two coats are needed, well rubbed down with steel wool.

Secure from somewhere a small corner ornament and take four squeezes in gesso pasta as described earlier, and fix them, just as before. Small corner ornaments are not easy to find on old frames, but they do exist. Sometimes a section of a larger corner ornament can be used, or a spandrel ornament from the face of a clock or from a piece of silverware. The ornaments should be steel-woolled and trimmed when they are dry and stained so that the colour can be closely matched and the entire frame waxed and polished with lambswool to give a restful antique glow.

If a light colour seems necessary, the wood can be left pale and the pasta tinted by mixing in a little yellow ochre to match the wood. After drying and steel-woolling, the entire frame can be waxed and polished. The effect is still period but, somehow, fresh with a gesture towards modern decor.

Small corner ornaments are extremely useful and can sometimes be found on late 19th-century photograph frames and the like. Frequently, from those eclectic times, the frame, though redolent of Queen Victoria retired to Osborne, or a saucy calf from the Moulin Rouge, contained elements that are purely classical or rococo. These should be garnered and stored whenever possible. The illustration shows an Italian engraving stained dark brown and treated by this simple means.

An 18th-century Italian engraving in a simple scooped frame with small corner ornaments such as were used in old private libraries and studies. The engraving is of Roman actors taken from an antique fresco or mosaic

GLAZING AND COMPLETION

GLAZED FRAMES should be made to fit the mount, never the reverse. Although the completed frame should be a unity of design comprizing picture, mount or matt and frame, in effect the frame has to be made to fit the mount. Glass (18 oz/500 g) is best cut in the glaziers. It is difficult to store in large sheets domestically and is not very economic in limited amounts. For measurement it should be about $\frac{1}{16}$ inch (1·5 mm) smaller than the frame. Over-tight glass can snap in a dry warm room if shrinkage or warping occurs. It is useful to be able to cut a larger faulty piece of glass smaller, to trim it to a smaller frame or picture than was originally intended. For this, a table covered with baize or blanket is needed, and two T-squares, blunt-nosed pliers and a diamond or steel wheel-cutter. The glass must be clean.

T-squares can be made to any convenient length cheaply, and should be slightly longer than the longest cut you can envisage if you are cutting down from spare glass. Effective T-squares can be made from $1\frac{1}{2} \times \frac{1}{4}$-inch (38 × 6-mm) hardwood assembled to a T-shape and glued on one end at an angle of 90°. Plainly this must be accurate. They are used upsidedown, with the cross piece underneath the long bar. Drill a hole for hanging on a nail when not in use. Cement a length of dressmaker's tape-measure along the appropriate edge of each long bar. One T-square is used for length and one for breadth, although these are notional terms. The tape-measures should be checked against a ruler for accuracy since old ones stretch. Cut a little notch in the crossbar on both T-squares to enable the tool to get into the edge of the glass. If a wheel tool is used it should be kept in a jar of methyl alcohol or white spirit (naptha) to prevent rust.

In order to cut the glass, two sides of it should be at right angles. Set the T-square on these and move one against the other until they enclose the chosen size. Allow about $\frac{1}{8}$ inch (3 mm) for the thickness of the base of the glass cutter and check again to ensure that the T-squares are lying 90° true. Take away the horizontal T-square, hold the cutter between the index and middle fingers, balanced by the thumb, inclining slightly towards yourself and cut firmly and quickly from the top to the base of the glass. A cut sounds different from a scratch and must be learnt by practice, listen for a light hiss. A scratch is whiter and is sometimes discontinuous. Bring the cut over the edge of the table and press downwards sharply. Alternatively lay the cut over the long bar of the T-square and press sharply. All cuts are made completely across a given piece of glass. Measure up the other dimension with a T-square and cut again. Cuts near the edge of a sheet sometimes leave serrated fragments which can be removed with a pliers. Rub the rough edges with a carborundum stone.

We have seen how to make mouldings, simple and complex, and

Glass ready for cutting

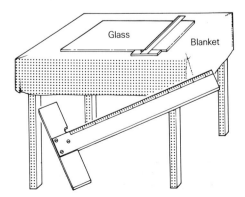

how to cut and assemble them into frame. Ready-made mouldings are cut and assembled similarly. We have also considered mounts (matts) for water-colours, engravings, drawings, lithographs, maps; in other words, artwork on paper which is always covered with glass and sealed from behind for atmospheric protection.

All pictures stretched over a window-mount need a rigid backing cut from mounting board, the same size as the window mount, or the glass for that matter. To finish off all such framing, clean the glass on both sides and lay it in the frame. Place the mounted picture on top of it, face down. The thickness of the window will prevent the picture touching the glass. Lay the backing card on the back of the mounted picture and be satisfied that everything fits. If the glass is slightly too small, but is still capable of covering the frame opening, a few fragments of matchstick, flicked with a contact cement, can be pressed between the edge of the glass and the rebate, where they will hold the glass in position. A few stamp-sized pieces of gummed tape from the back of the card to the back of the frame will do the same thing for a slightly undersized mount. I am talking of no more than ⅛ inch (3 mm) short measure, which sometimes happens, particularly at first. Before pinning the whole thing into the frame, make sure that no fragments of paper or wood are loose behind the glass.

To drive in the pins use a light hammer and ⅝-inch (16-mm) or ¾-inch (19-mm) moulding or veneer pins every four inches (100 mm) or so. Hold a block of wood (2 × 2 × 8 inches/50 × 50 × 200 mm) on the outside of the frame against the rebate, into which you are driving the pin. Lay the pin flat on the card and tap its point into the exposed piece of rebate. Do not drive it in at a descending angle. Drive the pins in about half-way and when they are all home, cover round this edge of the frame with strips of gummed paper, across the pins and onto the card, sealing the picture from anything except damp or excessive heat.

If a total and homogeneous seal is needed for the sake of appearance, a sheet of brown Kraft paper can be pasted over the entire back, frame and backing board with a strong cold water paste. Cut the paper a little larger than needed, paste the frame and backing board and also the paper and tamp the paper down. When dry it can be trimmed off

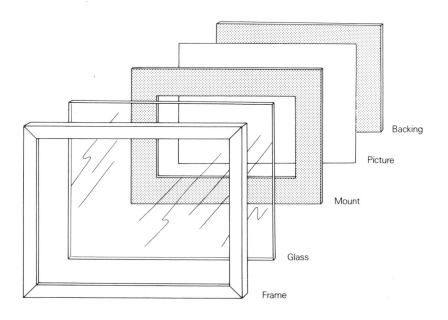

Backing

Picture

Mount

Glass

Frame

The sequence of components in a framed, mounted glazed picture. With oils, omit (usually) glass, mount and backing

A mounted picture before framing

The picture in its frame with backing board and pinning begun

with a knife or by rubbing the edge with a piece of fine sandpaper wrapped around a piece of cardboard 1 × 3 inches (25 × 75 mm), the surplus strips of paper will fall away.

Jobbing framers often use a kind of 'gun' which shoots thin flat diamond-shaped brads into the frame on squeezing a trigger, and anyone undertaking a lot of glazed framing might prefer one of these, but framers managed with pins for centuries before such useful tools were available.

Screw eyes, screw rings or D rings are used on the back of the frame to hold the hanging wire. Screw rings and screw eyes vary in size and heavier frames for oil paintings need large ones, about ½ inch (12 mm) in diameter. Start them with a thin awl and screw home, about one-third of the height down from the top. Use light or heavy

Apply gummed tape from the back of the frame on to the backing board and over the pins

The alcoholic return of Bacchus from India to hang above the port decanter

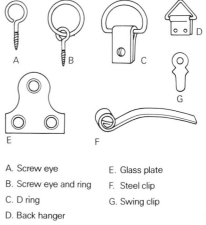

A. Screw eye
B. Screw eye and ring
C. D ring
D. Back hanger
E. Glass plate
F. Steel clip
G. Swing clip

(C) and (D) are rivitted to the backing board. (E) is for heavy mirrors. (F) is used for small oil canvasses for easy removal of painting. (G) Used mainly for photographs etc

brass-covered picture wire with about 1 inch (25 mm) looseness and always use it double, winding it round itself for a couple of inches to finish off.

D rings are useful when very narrow mouldings are used. These are often too fragile or shallow to take a screw eye. In this case, the backing piece should be cut from the thinnest hardboard and the D rings riveted to it. Nowadays they come in packets complete with rivets. The weight of the picture, glass and frame hang from the hardboard and does not strain the fragile mitres which narrow mouldings necessitate. Indeed, for large pictures with glass, narrow mouldings are dangerous. If self-effacement is needed in the frame, a somewhat wider moulding is safer, and reliance is placed on its texture and colour to keep in the background.

CONCLUSION

While I have covered the basics of framing in this book to the extent that an assiduous reader should be able to buy the tools and start mounting and framing, I have concentrated on areas of framing and making one's own mouldings not dealt with elsewhere.

Properly followed, it should enable the amateur or the professional to compete with gallery conservationists and bespoke framing experts reasonably well. Indeed, the scope is wider and less tied to conventional market demands. My greatest hopes are pinned on dedicated amateurs who can follow their obsession and devote time and research to the subject. The more of the latter the better.

It should be remembered also that many, though not all ornamented frames can be finished in a manner suitable for modern paintings. I have described thin wash colours over gesso and polyester glazes, but there is much more to be devised and invented. If I were to write this book in a year's time, doubtless the advice could be extended and I hope that some readers will assist in the enterprise, and perhaps I may see some of the results.

Modern moulding designs can be devised. I have used motifs based on Papuan bark cloth, seaweed and even sea surf on which to base rather flat moulding designs, working on flat strips of clay and casting onto wood.

The present movement in painting seems to point in towards the need for richer framing, and since industry seems unlikely to supply it in any aesthetically acceptable form, I hope this book will fill part of this need.

This frame is formed from the outer
moulding of a frame shown on page 43.
Within the picture there are two frames
shown, holding a mirror glass and a small
painting. Both are cast in Crystacal and
wax-gilded. On top is a frame cast from a
19th-century Italian moulding: a form of
rococo adapted to a repeating pattern and
pierced with holes to increase its enrichment
and lightness

INDEX

I wish to acknowledge courtesies and assistance from George Brandreth, Anne Dunlop and Cresten Doherty in the preparation of this book, and to offer gratitude to Tom Nisbet RHA, who sparked the quest long ago when every goose was a swan and every lass a queen. I am also indebted to many students of all ages whose needs and sympathy fired my energies.

PICTURE CREDITS

All black and white photography by Laurence Bradbury except 24, 92 top, 107.
Francis Lumley Front and back cover, 1, 25, 32/33, 64.
Rose Jones 2/3, 24, 36/37, 40, 49, 52/53, 60/61, 86/87, 90/91, 94/95, 99, 102/103, 107, 113.
Line drawings by Craig Austin and Phil Blakely.
Thanks to Blackman Harvey for supplying frames in 37 bottom and 102 top.